curious about

APPLE

BY RACHEL GRACK

AMICUS LEARNING

What are you

curious about?

CHAPTER THREE

Bet You Didn't Know...

PAGE
18

Curious About is published by
Amicus Learning, an imprint of Amicus
P.O. Box 227, Mankato, MN 56002
www.amicuspublishing.us

Editors: Ana Brauer and Grace Cain
Series Designer: Kathleen Petelinsek
Book Designer and Photo Researcher: Sara Hood

Library of Congress Cataloging-in-Publication Data
Names: Koestler-Grack, Rachel A., 1973- author.
Title: Curious about Apple / by Rachel Grack.
Description: Mankato, MN : Amicus Learning, an imprint of Amicus, [2026] | Series: Curious about favorite brands | Includes bibliographical references and index. | Audience term: Children | Audience: Ages 6–9 | Audience: Grades 2–3 | Summary: "Who invented Apple? Spark elementary readers' curiosity about the popular technology brand's history, products, and cultural impact with insightful questions and well-researched answers. Includes table of contents, glossary, further resources, and index"— Provided by publisher.
Identifiers: LCCN 2024050036 (print) | LCCN 2024050037 (ebook) | ISBN 9798892005098 (library binding) | ISBN 9798892005630 (paperback) | ISBN 9798892006170 (ebook)
Subjects: LCSH: Apple Computer, Inc.—Juvenile literature. | Computer industry—United States—Juvenile literature. | Brand name products—Juvenile literature.
Classification: LCC HD9696.2.U64 A67365 2026 (print) | LCC HD9696.2.U64 (ebook) | DDC 338.4/7004—dc23/eng/20241230
LC record available at https://lccn.loc.gov/2024050036
LC ebook record available at https://lccn.loc.gov/20

Photo Credits: Alamy Stock Photo/Alex Segre, 14, Lars Hagberg, 2, 17, Ryhor Bruyeu, 15, rvlsoft, 9; Getty Images/Archigram, 20–21, Facundo Diaz Montes, 16, JOHN G. MABANGLO, 12, Kimberly White, 7, shapecharge, 3, 19, SolStock, 11, Tom Munnecke, 9, Ulrich Baumgarten, 13; Shutterstock/Anton_Ivanov, 2, 6, Dennis MacDonald, 10, Kaspars Grinvalds, 15, Keshan De Mel, 15, Mike Mareen, 15, MohammadKam, 9, TonyV3112, 5, 19 STUDIO, 15; The Noun Project/achmad, 22, bsd studio, 23, Emmanuel Garcia Frias, 22, Rahmad romadoni, 23; Wikimedia Commons/Apple Computer, Inc., 8, Public Domain/Rob Janoff, cover, 1, 8, 9, Ronald Wayne, 8

Printed in India

CHAPTER ONE

What is Apple known for?

It is best known for making iPhones, iPads, and Macs. Apple products feature the newest **technology**. Most people find them easy to use. Apple is one of the biggest tech brands in the world!

The iPhone is Apple's most popular product.

The Apple IIe (2e) came out in 1983.

Who started Apple?

Steve Jobs and Steve Wozniak liked working with **electronics**. In 1976, they started building computers in a garage. They wanted to sell them to computer stores. Their friend Ronald Wayne helped set up the company. They called their computers Apples.

Steve Jobs (right) and Steve Wozniak met when they were teenagers.

DID YOU KNOW?
Ronald Wayne quickly sold his part of the company for $800. Today, it would be worth at least $60 billion.

Why did they pick the name Apple?

Some people think it had to do with Isaac Newton. He discovered gravity when an apple fell from a tree. Others say it is because of computer scientist Alan Turing. He died in 1954 after eating a poisoned apple. The real reason is simple. It was Jobs' favorite fruit.

APPLE LOGO THROUGH THE YEARS

1976

1977

1984

Jobs picked the name after visiting an orchard.

1998

2001

2007

2017

Why did Apple name its computer Mac?

McIntosh apples are known for their sweet flavor.

Macs are named after the McIntosh apple. This apple has a special flavor. Macs were special, too. They were the first computers with a mouse. Until 1984, people could only type commands to open menus. A mouse allows users to click on **icons**. Macs made using computers easy.

Macs are often used in classrooms.

CHAPTER TWO

Why do Apple products begin with "i"?

Jobs announced the first iMac on May 6, 1998.

The "i" stands for internet. Apple started the trend with the iMac in 1998. This desktop computer could easily connect to the internet. Using "i" became a catchy way to name Apple **smart devices**.

The first iMac was a huge hit. Apple sold more than six million of them!

What are MacBooks?

New MacBook models come out every year.

They are laptops. They open and close like a book. Get it? People use laptops on the go. They are thin and lightweight. This makes them easy to carry. Apple made the first laptops with a **trackpad**. This can be used instead of a mouse.

iPHONE
2007–NOW

iPAD
2010–NOW

MACBOOK
2006–NOW

iMAC
1998–NOW

APPLE WATCH
2015–NOW

What does an Apple Watch do?

People of all ages can use an Apple Watch.

An Apple Watch is like wearing a smartphone on your wrist. You can make calls, send a text, and check your email. The Apple Watch can also count your steps and track your heart rate. They help people stay fit and healthy.

You can keep track of workouts on your Apple Watch.

What other Apple products are there?

The iPad mini is popular. It can do almost anything an iPhone does. You can even make calls through iMessage or FaceTime. iTunes is also popular. You can buy music or movies directly from the **app**.

STREAMING SERVICE

Apple TV+ launched in 2019. It has hundreds of movies and shows available to watch. It even releases original content.

The App Store has countless games you can download and play.

Why is Apple so popular?

People love the way Apple products talk with each other. One person can put their information on multiple devices at once. Also, people can count on them to work well and last a long time. Apple links lives together with every product it makes.

FaceTime lets Apple users connect even when far away.

APPLE EVENTS

Apple holds an event to talk about new products before they come out. The events are watched by millions of people.

STAY CURIOUS!

ASK MORE QUESTIONS

How many people own iPhones?

What Apple products are coming out next?

Try a BIG QUESTION: What new technology could change everyday life?

SEARCH FOR ANSWERS

Search the library catalog or the Internet.
A librarian, teacher, or parent can help you.

Using Keywords
Find the looking glass.

Keywords are the most important words in your question.

If you want to know about:

- how many people own iPhones, type: IPHONE USERS IN THE WORLD
- new Apple products, type: APPLE EVENTS

LEARN MORE

FIND GOOD SOURCES

Here are some good, safe sources you can use in your research.
Your librarian can help you find more.

Books

Apple
by Sara Green, 2024.

Steve Jobs: Computer Pioneer & Co-Founder of Apple
by Grace Hansen, 2020.

Internet Sites

Ducksters: Steve Jobs
https://www.ducksters.com/biography/entrepreneurs/steve_jobs.php
Ducksters is an educational site for kids with information on a variety of topics.

Kiddle: Apple Inc. Facts for Kids
https://kids.kiddle.co/Apple_Inc.
Kiddle is an online encyclopedia for kids.

Every effort has been made to ensure that these websites are appropriate for children. However, because of the nature of the Internet, it is impossible to guarantee that these sites will remain active indefinitely or that their contents will not be altered.

SHARE AND TAKE ACTION

Purchase a computer kit.
Ask a friend to help put it together.

Pick an Apple device.
Think of ways to make it better or easier to use.

Talk about technology with a friend.
Come up with a list of electronic devices you would build.

GLOSSARY

app A computer program designed for phones and other small devices.

electronics Technology that uses electricity to run.

icon Pictures or symbols used on electronic devices.

smart device Electronic equipment that connects to the internet.

technology A branch of study that deals with science and engineering.

trackpad A touchpad on a laptop used instead of a mouse.

INDEX

About the Author

Rachel Grack has been editing and writing children's books since 1999. She lives on a small ranch in southern Arizona. As a lover of stories, Disney is close to her heart. She also enjoys watching her grandchildren play Pokémon games on her Nintendo 64 console.